DaddyTeller:

Be a Hero to Your Kids
and Teach Them What's Really Important
by Telling One Simple Story at a Time.

DaddyTeller:

Be a Hero to Your Kids
and Teach Them What's Really Important
by Telling One Simple Story at a Time.

Written By
K. Sean Buvala
www.seantells.net

DaddyTeller:

Be a Hero to Your Kids and Teach Them What's Really Important by Telling One Simple Story at a Time.

©2009 K. Sean Buvala
ISBN 978-0-557-13160-0

Published by:

Creation Company Consultants
PO Box 392 Tolleson, AZ 85353
www.storyteller.net
www.twitter.com/daddyteller

Dedicated To:

My children who have heard
many stories from me
for so very long
that now they say
"tell me a story but only tell the funny parts."

Some Other Projects by Sean Buvala

Ebook:
The Storytelling 101 Training Kit
www.storytelling101.com

CD Recordings

"Calling Out a Rising Sun: Stories for Teenage Guys"
"Seven Ravens: Unvarnished Tales from the Brothers Grimm"
"Serengeti Stories: Wisdom Tales of the Animals" (Coming Soon)

www.1800buymycd.com

DaddyTeller

www.daddyteller.com

Acknowledgements

Thanks to the many people who make a project like this work including my editing/proofreading team of my family and friends including Michelle, Helgar, Patricia and Ken; my wife Michelle (aka "the proofreader") who allows me to create these projects; my children who tell me that if they had a choice they'd take a storytelling poppa over just about any other job I could have; Stephan Stavrakis who helped me think of this project in a new light; to the storytelling communities both online at Storyteller.net and live in-person in Arizona who keep me on my toes as I try to create new and exciting things in the storytelling world; to the many Dads who have said to me, "I wish I knew how to do that storytelling thing with *my* kids."

Table of Contents

Wait!

Let's make it 9 stories!

This book is only the beginning of the DaddyTeller™ program! For more updates, some free stories, audio commentary, workshop dates, coaching and more, come to the website at:

http://www.daddyteller.com/extrabook
The page password is: mouselion2apple

Today, register at the website to receive our Email updates. Then check your Email for a confirmation request! When you confirm your registration, you will get a link to an additional free story as well as other bonus items.

Don't delay- do this while you are thinking about it. Join our community at:

http://www.daddyteller.com/extrabook
The page password is: mouselion2apple

We will not sell, rent or distribute your Email to anyone. Your privacy is important to us.

Introduction

Hey Dad,[1]

You are about to become a hero.

It's time for you to reconnect with your kids[2]. You know you are probably missing out on their lives.

Studies say that the average father spends less than 30 minutes per day in conversation with his kids, yet kids spend dozens of hours per week in front of the TV or video games.[3] Twenty-seven minutes of Dad time per day vs. 2400 minutes of TV time per week? How much time do you spend with your kids? What's your conversation time like? By the way, the yelling about "take out the trash" and "don't eat like a pig" does not count in those 30 minutes.

You want to teach your kids and you want to share your values. You are looking for your sons to know the real values that make up being well-rounded men. You want your daughters to be independent, smart women.

You can do this, but you must open your mouth. You can pass on your values, but you have to start talking.

You can teach your child about a virtue or value at bedtime tonight and have them wake up tomorrow morning as different people.

Stop fearing that "I don't know what to say." As your coach, I am about to teach you what to say. Don't worry that "I will sound stupid." I'll suggest ways for you to tell the story, because even the slightest amount of confidence you have translates into big confidence to your child.

You are about to be brilliant. You are about to take part in the education of your own children.

You are about to achieve all this through the power of storytelling.

Storytelling?! Hold on, there, Dad. I didn't say you are going to read books in that sing-songy librarian voice. You are going to talk like the man you are.

You are not going to have to learn the ins and outs of acting and theater. You are about to give a gift to your child, one of just being you, in your voice and with your own abilities.

Let's get you started getting closer to your kids. You can begin right now.

Choose a value lesson from this book. Read the story. Use my "Brick-and-Mortar Story Reminders"™ I wrote for you.

Sit down with your kids.

Look them in the eye and tell them a story with no book or props to get in your way. Do your best. This isn't a contest for crying out loud.

You are about to become a hero.

Go, Dad, Go! I know you are going to do a great job.

Wishing you the best times with your children,

-Sean

Chapter One

Quick-start, ten-step get-started guide.

I want you to be able to dive in to telling stories to your children. For that, here's the quick instructions on how to use this book. You can (and should) go more in-depth later by going through chapter two.

I know that you want to jump in, like a sixteen-year-old with his first driver's license. You remember those days, don't you? I hope you are as excited about relating to and connecting with your children as you were back on that day.

1. Choose the value lesson you would most like to share with your child.

This book is broken up into chapters, with a value or teaching in each chapter. For this volume one, we have chosen to focus on the values of honesty, integrity, kindness, self-worth and the dangers of greed. We'll give you many more values in future volumes of this DaddyTeller™ series.

2. Select a story you would like to tell.

Take a quick look at all the stories in this book. For the easiest story to tell, look at "The Lion and the Mouse" in Chapter 7. Choose this story or any other story to start.

3. Read the story to yourself six times.

Yes, six times. You can do that. Who cares how long it takes you- this isn't a race and you have nothing to prove. You'll spend more time reading the newspaper (or your smart phone) in the bathroom than you will reading these stories six times.

4. Read the second version of the story that includes [my storytelling coach's know-how notes] to you.

In the second version of the story I will include some coaching notes about how you can customize this story. **[you'll find these notes in brackets like these]**

5. Now, read the story aloud to yourself several times.

If you have an office, shut the door and read the story aloud. Hear yourself speak the words. If you don't have an office, then go sit in your car and read the story to yourself. Do this at least four times in a row. Take your time and ignore any strange looks you get while you are talking to yourself. You are going to be a hero to your kid and a few quizzical looks aren't going to kill you. Read aloud and customize the story if you want by [using the notes I have included for you.] [4]

6. Take a look at the "Brick and Mortar Story Reminder"™ list for the story.

I have broken every story down for you into the episodes of the story. You can see each sentence reminding you of what happens first, second, third and so on.

7. Using just the "Brick-and-Mortar Story Reminder"™ list, tell (out loud) the story to yourself.

It's okay if you leave out some parts as long as you make sense. Unlike baseball, you can skip a base and still get home in storytelling. Bonus: if you have a way to record yourself, do it. Video or audio is just fine. Then go back and listen. Don't worry about what your "voice sounds like." You can be sure that your kids love to hear your voice.

8. If you need notes, write the "Brick-and-Mortar Story Reminder"™ list on a small piece of paper.

If you need to, write out (yes, your hand with a pen/pencil and some paper) the summary as your quick reminders of the order of the story. Handwriting this will help lock the story in your brain.

9. Tell your story to your child.

For most of these stories, we are assuming that you are telling them to children from the cradle to about 10 years old. In a future book, I'll teach you about telling to tweens and teens. However, with young children, sit on the bed with your kid or together on the couch. Sit close, look your kid in the eyes and tell the story you have been working on. It's okay if you get a step wrong or forget something- just stop and do some back fill.

10. At the end of the story, if you are telling to a child old enough to speak, close your mouth and listen to what your kid has to say.

At the end of the story, you might ask after a few moments of silence, "Why do you think the mouse (or any character in the story) acted like that?" After your children and you discuss their interpretation, feel free to add your own short comments. Don't worry, you don't have to teach it all in one night. Your kids are going to ask for their favorite stories over and over again. Here's a hint: the stories that they want to hear repeated are the tales that their little minds have subconsciously decided they need to hear.

Congrats, Daddy Hero,
you are on your way to making
a huge impact on your kids.

Chapter Two

What to Expect in Being a DaddyTeller™ Father

When you tell stories, you will be more interesting, entertaining and educational to your kids than any amusement park anywhere.

I have been a full-time professional storyteller for nearly a quarter of a century. In those 25 years, I have performed for audiences of thousands and audiences of just a few people. I teach storytelling to major business and non-profit groups. I know story and how stories are best presented in most situations.

However, I have the most fun when my own children are laughing at the stories we tell to each other. I know you will experience this same joy when you tell the stories in this book (and the volumes to come) to your children.

I wrote this DaddyTeller™ series to help you connect with your kids. If I could talk to each man who is reading this book, I would start by telling you about how important your role is in the life of your child. I would tell you to not be afraid or self-conscious about telling stories to your babies, even if those babies are now ten years old.

Your child wants to interact with you, with your unique mannerisms and your unique way of talking. To your young children, you are the hero. You are privileged to be called by a pet name: Dad, Father, Papa, Abba, Da, Pops, Padre, Daddy or whatever word is used in your household[5]. In my house, it's Poppa.

In no special order, here are ten tips, tricks and thoughts about storytelling with children.

1. Look your children in the eye. Tell these stories, don't read them.

Put the book down, tell the story as you look at your kids. You created these beautiful children. How often do you actually look at them? This is your chance.

In the first chapter, I have listed for you the process of learning to tell stories. If you haven't read that chapter yet, stop for a moment and go read it. "Telling" means that you do not use the book. It also means that you do not memorize the story! The story comes from your head and imagination right into the eager ears of your children.

After each story, I have given you my unique "Brick-and-Mortar Storytelling Summary"™ so that you can remember the story step by step. Then, I have repeated the story for you along with my coaching notes about telling the story **[enclosed in brackets like this.]** Use those bold, bracketed notes, which I have kept very simple, to add some details, fun or uniqueness to the way you will tell the story.

2. Your children will ask you to repeat these stories.

That is normal and good. **The** learning of the values comes from repetition. If you were part of any organized sports or extra-curricular activity in school, then you know the value of repeating a play, a speech, a chess game or other focused activity. I have learned that when your child asks for the same story over and over again, there is something that they are trying to learn about life or themselves from that story. Try to avoid saying, "You want to hear that story again?" Be honored that they're asking you to be the bearer of story and values.

3. Change the genders, names or any other details in the stories if you want.

You are telling these stories for *your* children. Do you want to make "The Girl in the Forest" be "The Boy in the Forest?" Go ahead! Maybe you want the apples brought to the prince by the youngest daughter of the woman who owns the farm. Do what you want with these stories.

Maybe you are uncomfortable with calling the helper in "The Woodcutter's Decision" a "water spirit." That is okay. Make it a magic sea-horse or an angel from above or a scuba-diving robot. Again, *you* are in charge of the story. Aesop, the Grimm Brothers and I will not be offended. You even get an "atta boy" from me for really focusing on what you need to do for your children.

In these stories, I have not named the characters. You can do that if you wish. You can have the main characters just happen to have the same name as your child, if you want. You can name anyone in the stories whatever you'd like to name them. Enjoy the process.

4. Heads Up: Your kid will start to "own" these stories.

Part of the internalizing process I mentioned above includes children becoming confident in the rhythm of the story. For children, who don't really have the control of "what comes next" in their lives, the assurance of the same pattern in the stories you tell is comforting to them. Since you are telling the story and not reading or memorizing it, there will be subtle differences each time you tell it. That is okay, too. After they have heard a story a few times, your child will tell you if you get something out of order.

Here's a bonus benefit to your storytelling: children who hear and learn stories develop better math skills, too! Stories contain sequence, patterns, organization and logical thinking.

Those are all skills children need to understand math. Congratulations, Dad! You are passing on values and teaching math at the same time. This is like getting two parenting books in one.

5. Take your time and play with the stories

The world folktales I have included in this volume have been around longer than any of us. One of the reasons for that is because they are entertaining. It is your job to please have fun with these stories.

Don't rush through them. Make some goofy voices. Talk loudly when the characters in the story are talking loud. Speak very softly when you are speaking as small creatures. For fun, switch voices sometimes so the tiny mouse talks like the big lion, for example.

Make words sound like what they mean. For example, in the story of "The Ant and the Dove," the word "bit" towards the end of the sentence should be a quick, big and surprising sound. For the most part, when you tell stories to your child, go for funny over too serious.

Play with how fast or how slow the different characters speak. In "The Fisherman and His Wife" story, the exchange between the fish and the fisherman probably gets a little faster and frustrating (to the characters) each time they talk. In "The Girl in the Forest" story, the kind sister might talk with more gentleness than the rude sister does. Just play.

6. A story told with bumps and mistakes is better than not telling at all.

Making mistakes is a part of the process when interacting with your children. Don't wait to be perfect before telling stories to your kids.

As you get more comfortable, your confidence and your ability to quickly learn and tell stories will grow. Even if the very first story you choose to tell to your children comes within hours of buying this book, you are not going to fail. You are doing a great thing for your children and there is no judgment on your success. This isn't your high-school basketball or debate-team finals where there is only one chance for success and glory. Your gift to your kids is the attention you are giving them and the life-lessons you are teaching them.

You might be worried about skipping some details when you tell the story. That's nothing to worry about, professional storytellers miss details all the time. Just add them in when you need them.

For example, in the story of "The Girl in the Forest," You might forget in the beginning to say that she takes the snacks with her when she leaves her house. That is okay. When you get to the part where the girl takes out her lunch, you can just say something simple such as, "Wasn't she a smart girl for remembering to pack snacks for herself before she left?"

7. Switch gears and ask your kids to tell these stories (or any stories) back to you.

After you have told these stories to your children for some time, ask them to tell the stories back to you. As they learn stories with you, you can "trade off" stories, with you telling a story and your child telling the story back to you. Some nights, ask your child for a bedtime story. They'll learn reading and writing skills such as vocabulary building, critical thinking, abstraction, structuring and use of imagination. This is surprise number two, Dad! Your storytelling now helps your child to learn the language arts! You are going to make your child's teacher very proud of you as you practice these "literacy" skills with your child.

What a great investment this book is for you and your children. And you thought you were just buying a book of stories for bedtime. . .

8. Tell stories to your little kids so they will remember the lessons when they're teens.

Stories teach values in a non-threatening way and without a heavy-handed lecture. The repetition of the stories in this book helps you to emphasize the importance of the values of kindness, self-worth, honesty, personal integrity and the dangers of greed. When, in the future, your teenager is going mad for the latest and greatest gadget, you can remind him of the problem of greed "in that story of the fisherman I used to tell you." When your teenage child tries too hard to do all the wrong things that all her peers are doing, then you will be able to remind her of the story of the donkey who wanted to be a lion.

9. Come get an extra story for your child today by visiting the www.daddyteller.com website.

Keep in touch with us! Visit daddyteller.com/extrabook to sign up for our Email list. When you do that, you will be rewarded with a link to download one more story (with all the DaddyTeller™ features) that was not included in this book. We might even throw in another surprise. Come register today while you are thinking about it.

10. Grow your communication skills even more when you get the Storytelling 101 EWorkbook.

I designed an Ebook training course to teach anyone how to create and tell stories. If you would like to learn more about in-depth storytelling techniques for your family and your career field, please stop by and order your personal copy of the EBook at www.storytelling101.com

Chapter Three

The Woodcutter's Decision

Honesty and Integrity

Background

This story is an adaptation of a very old fable. It is a simple and easy story for you to remember.[6]

The Story

Once there was a woodcutter who had an iron axe. It was not the most-perfect looking axe that anyone had ever seen.

However, the woodcutter cared for the axe as it had been handed down to him from his father and his father before him.

Although the woodcutter was a very good woodcutter, times were hard and some days he did not make enough money to pay all his bills. Still, he was happy to be doing a job he loved.

One day, while he was chopping wood near a lake, his hands got all sweaty and the axe slipped away from his hands and sunk to the bottom of the lake. The woodcutter realized he had now lost his way to make his living as well as an important gift his father had given him.

He was so shocked at the loss of his axe that he began to cry out to the heavens for help. As he did so, a water-spirit rose from the lake and asked the woodcutter why he was so upset.

"I have lost my axe in the water," he said.

The water-spirit said to him, "Wait here and I will go get it for you." With a splash, the water-spirit dove down to the bottom of the lake.

A few moments later, the water-spirit came to the surface with an axe made of pure silver in her hands. The woodcutter had never seen such a valuable axe before. He knew if he took the axe and sold it, all of his money problems would be solved.

She looked at the woodcutter and asked him, "Is this your axe that you lost?"

Although he wanted to say yes, he chose to be honest. "No," said the woodcutter, "that is not my axe."

The water-spirit again dove down into the water and returned with an axe made of pure gold. Although this axe was worth even more than the first, the honest woodcutter said no when she asked if it was his. Being honest was a very difficult decision for him.

Finally, she dove into the water one more time. When she came back up, she had in her hands the woodcutter's iron axe.

She said to him, "Woodcutter, is this simple axe the axe you lost?"

"Yes," the relieved Woodcutter said, "that is the axe I lost. Thank you for finding it for me."

The water-spirit then handed the iron axe to the woodcutter and told him to stay where he was as she would return in just a moment. She dove into the water and returned with both the gold and silver axes in her hands.

"Because you were honest with me, I will reward you with these gifts. Take them and live a long happy life," she said as she handed the axes to the woodcutter.

When the honest woodcutter returned home, many people asked about his good luck. He told them what had happened. Unfortunately, one of his neighbors was jealous and dishonest.

The dishonest neighbor went to his tool shed and grabbed an old axe. He then went to the side of the very same lake and threw it into the water. While he was pretending to cry, the water-spirit emerged from the lake with an axe of gold.

"Woodcutter, is this the axe that you have lost?" she asked him while looking deep into his eyes.

"Yes, oh yes!" cried the greedy neighbor as he reached out to take the axe of gold away from the water-spirit.

However, she held back the axe and told him that she knew he was lying and that he was being dishonest and greedy.

She said to him, "Because you could not be honest, I will not give you this axe nor will I go and get your real axe. You may sit here by the edge of the lake and regret your dishonesty."

And with those words, she dove back into the water and vanished. The dishonest neighbor sat by the lake and, this time, cried real tears.

However, the woodcutter lived every day of his life in joy and peace, happy with his decision to be always honest.

Your "Brick-And-Mortar Story Reminder"™ List

1. Woodcutter (WC) has family axe with family meaning
2. WC chops wood by lake and axe slips from hand into water
3. WC is upset and does not know what to do
4. Water spirit (WS) rises from water and asks what is wrong
5. WS dives into water and returns with silver axe
6. WC says axe is not his
7. WS dives into water and returns with gold axe
8. WC says axe is not his
9. WS dives into water and returns with original axe
10. WC takes family axe
11. WS dives into water and returns with gold and silver axe
12. Dishonest neighbor (DN) finds out the Story

13. DN goes to lake, throws in his axe, and pretends to cry.
14. WS offers him a golden axe
15. DN tries to take golden axe
16. WS will not give axe for DN was not honest
17. WS vanishes and DN left with nothing.

My Coaching Notes for You

Once there was a woodcutter **[you might have to tell your child what a woodcutter does]** **[the woodcutter's name could be the name of your child- remember to change the genders if you want to]** who had an iron axe. It was not the most perfect-looking axe that anyone had ever seen. However, the woodcutter cared for the axe as it had been handed down to him from his father and his father **[it could be mother to mother]** before him.

Although the woodcutter was a very good woodcutter, times were hard and some days he did not make enough money to pay all his bills. Still, he was happy to be doing a job he loved.

One day, while he was chopping wood near a lake, his hands got all sweaty and the axe slipped away from his hands and sunk to the bottom of the lake **[during this sentence you can make the gestures of chopping wood and show how the axe slipped away from his hands]**. The woodcutter realized he had now lost his way to make his living as well as an important gift his father had given him.

He was so shocked at the loss of his axe that he began to cry out **[raise your hands towards the heavens to beg for help]** to the heavens for help. As he did so, a water-spirit rose from the lake **[look out as if you are looking at the river and use your eyes and hands to show the water-spirit rising from the lake]** and asked the woodcutter why he was so upset.

"I have lost my axe in the water," he said.

The water-spirit said to him, "Wait here and I will go get it for you." With a splash [make a sound like water splashing], the water-spirit dove down to the bottom of the lake.

A few moments later, the water-spirit came to the surface with an axe made of pure silver [describe the axe with awe in your voice] in her hands. The woodcutter had never seen such a valuable axe before. He knew if he took that axe and sold it, all of his money problems would be solved.

She looked at the woodcutter and asked him, "Is this your axe that you lost?"[ask your child what they think the woodcutter should do]

Although he wanted to say yes, he chose to be honest. "No," said the woodcutter, "that is not my axe."

The water-spirit again dove down into the water [splash!] and returned with an axe made of pure gold [again describe this axe with awe and wonder in your voice]. Although this axe was worth even more than the first, the honest woodcutter said no when she asked if it was his. Being honest was a very difficult decision for him.

Finally, she dove into the water [splash!] one more time. When she came back up, she had in her hands [be sure to gesture as if you are holding out this axe] the woodcutter's iron axe.

She said to him, "Woodcutter, is this simple axe the axe you lost?"

"Yes," the relieved [show the relief in your voice] Woodcutter said, "that is the axe I lost. Thank you for finding it for me."

The water-spirit then handed the iron axe [reach out to take the axe] to the woodcutter and told him to stay where he was as she would return in just a moment. She dove into the water [splash] and returned with both the gold and silver axes in her hands.

"Because you were honest with me, I will reward you with these gifts. Take them and live a long happy life," she said as she handed the axes to the woodcutter.

When the honest woodcutter returned home, many people asked about his good luck. He told them what had happened. Unfortunately, one of his neighbors was jealous and dishonest.

The dishonest neighbor went to his tool shed and grabbed an old axe. He then went to the side of the very same lake and threw it into the water. While he was pretending to cry [use some silly, pretend crying here], the water-spirit emerged from the lake with an axe of gold.

"Woodcutter, is this the axe that you have lost?" she asked him while looking deep into his eyes.

"Yes, oh yes!" [your voice should show his fake sincerity] cried the greedy neighbor as he reached out [he should reach out with trembling hands] to take the axe of gold away from the water-spirit.

However, she held back the axe [she should quickly snatch back the axe to keep it from him] and told him that she knew he was lying and that in his heart he was dishonest and greedy.

She said to him, "Because you could not be honest, I will not give you this axe nor will I go and get your real axe. You may sit here by the edge of the lake and regret your dishonesty."

And with those words, she dove back into the water [splash!} and vanished. The dishonest neighbor sat by the lake and cried real tears.

However, the woodcutter lived every day of his life in joy and peace, happy with his decision to be always honest.

Chapter Four

The Donkey Who Thought
He Was a Lion

Honesty, Integrity and Self Worth

Background

I have changed this common fable[7] to be a fun way to teach your children about the importance of being genuine with everyone they meet.

The Story

 A long time ago, when the animals could speak to each other, there lived a donkey who worked very hard. However, he was not happy being a donkey for he sometimes felt ignored. It seemed, to him anyway, that no one ever paid attention to him. Whether that was true or not, that was how the donkey felt.

One day, when the donkey was out running about the fields, he saw before him a huge field patch of bright yellow flowers growing near a lake. He thought to himself that he would love to eat the flowers, as he never had such a treat before.

The donkey ran to the flowers and rolled about in them as he munched, covering himself in yellow pollen. When he saw his reflection in the lake, he thought that he now looked golden like a lion.

He then stuck his head deep into the patch of flowers and twisted his neck about, wrapping the yellow flowers and stems about his neck. When he looked into the water this time, he saw that the flowers about his neck looked like the mane of a great, fierce lion.

"Now, everyone will be afraid of me since I look like a dangerous lion. They won't ignore me now!" he thought to himself as he made his way back to the village.

When the people and animals of the village saw the donkey coming down the road, they thought a real lion was heading right toward their homes. They ran away to their homes, screaming and crying out.

The donkey was pleased with his newfound power. When he arrived at the village, all the people and animals had run away and were hiding, except for one little duck, who sat in the middle of the road.

The donkey yelled at the duck. "Do you not fear me? I am a mean lion!" To prove his point, the donkey tried to make a great roar, but all that came out was:

"HEE HAW! HEE HAW!"

The duck just blinked his eyes and said to the donkey, "You are silly. For no matter how much you pretend to be something you are not, your voice will always give you away!"

When the inhabitants of the village saw and heard the fake lion, they all rushed from their homes and poured bucket after bucket of cold water on the donkey, washing away his yellow mane and color.

From that day on, they always thought the donkey was the silliest (and most dishonest) animal ever.

Your "Brick-And-Mortar Story Reminder"™ List

1. Donkey is not happy being a donkey
2. Donkey out playing in fields sees yellow flowers to eat
3. Donkey rolls in flower as he eats; gets covered in pollen
4. Donkey sees his yellow reflection in lake; decides to be lion
5. Donkey wraps flowers around neck to make a mane
6. Donkey heads toward town thinking all will fear him
7. People and animals run away as the "lion" comes toward them
8. Little Duck sits in middle of road
9. Donkey questions duck and tells duck to be afraid
10. Donkey tries to roar but only hee-haw comes out
11. Duck says the voice gives away who the Donkey really is
12. Villagers pour cold water on Donkey to wash away pollen

My Coaching Notes for You

A long time ago, when the animals could speak to each other, there lived a donkey **[although I have encouraged you to change the names of characters, I would not name this donkey after your child]** who worked very hard. However, he was not happy **[big sigh here]** being a donkey for he sometimes felt ignored. It seemed, to him anyway, that no one ever paid attention to him. Whether that was true or not, that was how the donkey felt.

One day, when the donkey was out running about the fields, he saw before him **[point out to the patch of flowers]** a huge field patch of bright yellow flowers growing near a lake. He thought to himself that he would love to eat the flowers **[show excitement here as the donkey thinks he will get a tasty lunch]**, as he never had such a treat before.

The donkey ran to the flowers and rolled [use your shoulders and upper body to show rolling around] about in them as he munched [make munching sounds with your mouth], covering himself in yellow pollen. When he saw his reflection in the lake, he thought that he now looked golden like a lion.

He then stuck his head deep into the patch of flowers and twisted his neck about [show this action with your head and neck], wrapping the yellow flowers and stems about his neck. When he looked into the water this time, he saw that the flowers about his neck looked like the mane of a [slowly build up the next words] great, fierce lion.

"Now, everyone will be afraid of me since I look like a dangerous lion. They won't ignore me now!" [use a big growling voice as the donkey pretends to be powerful] he thought to himself as he made his way back to the village.

When the people and animals of the village saw the donkey coming down the road [you could use your hands and body to show how the donkey walks now that he thinks he is a lion], they thought a real lion was heading right toward their homes. They ran away [talk quickly here as the people run away] to their homes, screaming and crying out [you can use some play screaming here].

The donkey was pleased with his newfound power. When he arrived at the village, all the people and animals had run away and were hiding, except for one little duck [remember with small children the description of the size of the duck is important- so emphasize it], who sat right in the middle of the road.

The donkey yelled [again use the fake powerful voice of the donkey- this is a funny scene so be a bit silly] at the duck. "Do you not fear me? I am a mean lion!" To prove his point, the donkey tried to make a great roar, but all that came out was:

"HEE HAW! HEE HAW!"[the more you give to making this goofy sound, the more your child will enjoy it]

The duck just blinked his eyes [again, a funny scene where you should take a few slow blinks while looking right at your child] and said to the donkey [duck must look up to the donkey], "You are silly. For no matter how much you pretend to be something you are not, your voice will always give you away!"[think about how this little duck might sound and make that voice- you won't do it wrong]

When the inhabitants of the village saw and heard the fake lion, they all rushed from their homes and poured bucket after bucket of cold water on the donkey [make the donkey shiver and shake in a funny way], washing away his yellow mane and color.

From that day on, they always thought the donkey was the silliest (and most dishonest) animal ever.

Chapter Five

The Girl in the Forest

Kindness

Background

Use this story when you want to talk about the power of serving others. I have adapted this story from a much longer story from the 1800's. This story might be best to tell to your older child. [8]

The Story

A long time ago, when the world was a much simpler place, a little girl went for a walk in the woods. Now, today you would never walk alone in the forest, but back in the time of this story, you could. She took bread and jelly for her snack and put it in her sack.

As she walked along, she did not pay attention to where she was going and soon became lost. As night fell, she was afraid she would never get home. Just then, she looked ahead and saw a light in the forest. As she moved towards it, she saw that it was a small house.

She went to the house and knocked on the door. When the door opened, she saw standing before her an old grandmother-woman. The girl asked the woman, "I am so lost. Can you help me?"

"Of course I will, child. Come in from the cold!" said the old woman.

When the girl entered the house, she sat down next to the fire. She opened up her sack to eat her meal.

"Oh," said the old woman, "I have not eaten much today. Would you share your snack with me?'

The little girl agreed and said, "Here, take what you want and I will eat what is left over."

When the grandmother had eaten some of the food, the girl ate her portion of the bread and jelly. There was even some left over.

"Well," said the kindly old woman, "it is not safe for you to go back out into the darkness to find your way home. You should stay here for the night. You may sleep in my soft bed in my room and I will sleep out here on some straw on the floor."

"No, I will take the straw and you can stay in your soft bed. Your old bones deserve a soft place to sleep," the girl responded.

So they slept the night away. When the girl woke up in the morning, she could not find the old woman anywhere. However, at the front door, there was a large sack of gold coins and a note attached to it.

The note read, "Dear Child, I am an enchanted fairy who needed someone to be kind to her. Because of your kindness, I have given you this bag of gold. On the other side of this note, you will find the map to guide you out of the forest. Thank you and live a long happy life."

The girl took the map and the gold and set out to her home. When she arrived at her house, her family was happy to see that she was safe and sound. She told them the story of what had happened and showed them the bag of gold.

Her sister heard this story and was very jealous. So, she packed up a bag of delicious snacks and set out to find the old woman's house.

As night fell, the sister found the old woman's house, with the light from the fire shining through the windows. The sister banged on the door.

When the old woman answered, the sister demanded to be let in. The old woman agreed.

The sister then began to eat her snacks. As before, the old woman asked to have some of the meal. The sister replied, "I have been walking all day and I am very hungry. You can have what is left over."

However, the sister was rude and she ate nearly every last piece of the snacks, leaving just crumbs and bits left for the old woman.

When it was time for bed, the old woman again offered to sleep on the straw while the sister could have the bed. Then, without even a concern for the old woman's weary body, the sister ran to the bedroom, slammed the door and slept all night on the soft bed, while the old woman had to sleep on the straw.

In the morning, the rude sister was eager to see her reward. Of course, the old woman was gone, but the sister could not care less about that. On the floor was a note and very small bag. The rude sister grabbed the note to read it.

"Dear child," the note began, "I have put the map on the back of this note to guide you back home. As well, you will find the reward that you deserve in this small sack. You should open it at once!"

When the rude sister opened the bag, there was no gold inside of it. Instead, there was bird with a sharp beak, which flew out of the bag and grabbed the sister's nose. The bird pulled harder and harder and the girl's nose stretched longer and longer. It pulled so hard that her nose hung all the way down to her feet. Then the bird vanished, leaving the sister with the long nose.

The long-nosed sister made her way home, tripping over her nose and being laughed at by everyone she passed, each laugh reminding her how she had been so mean to the old woman.

When she arrived home and shared her story, her family was shocked and amazed at her misfortune. However, as time went by the girl who acted with kindness taught her rude sister how to be kind. With each act of kindness she performed, her nose shrank just a little bit, until one day, her nose was as normal as normal could be.

So they all lived, kindly ever after.

Your "Brick-And-Mortar Story Reminder"™ List

1. Girl takes snacks, walks through forest, gets lost
2. She finds small house and knocks on door
3. Old Woman (OW) invites her in.
4. Girl opens her snacks, OW asks to share, girl agrees
5. OW tells girl to sleep on bed, OW to sleep on straw
6. Girl refuses bed, sleeps on straw
7. Next morning girl wakes up, OW is gone
8. Girl finds bag of money, note and map
9. Note tells girl that OW was fairy, kindness pays off
10. Rude sister (RS) hears girl's story and sets off to find house
11. RS finds house, knocks on door, OW admits girl
12. RS will not share meal and sleeps on soft bed
13. Next morning, RS finds small bag, note and map
14. Note tells RS that her "reward" is in the bag
15. RS opens bag, small bird flies out and stretches RS's nose
16. RS returns home, over time nose shrinks as she becomes kind

My Coaching Notes for You

A long **[don't get discouraged at the length of this story as it follows a pattern- don't forget to have fun and be playful when telling this story]** time ago, when the world was a much simpler place, a little girl went for a walk in the woods. **[you can change the genders of the characters to boys if you want]** Now, today you would never walk alone in the forest, but back in the time of this story, you could. **[it is a good idea to include this little reminder]** She took bread and jelly **[pretend to put food in a sack]** for her snack and put it in her sack.

As she walked along, she did not pay attention to where she was going **[let this be funny as you look around and daydream as you speak]** and soon became lost. As night fell, she was afraid she would never get home. Just then, she looked ahead and saw a light in the forest **[show relief by making the "whew!" sound and wiping your forehead]**. As she moved towards it, she saw that it was a small house.

She went to the house and knocked on the door **[pretend to knock on door and maybe make a sound like knocking]** When the door opened **[go ahead and make a funny creaking sound]**, she saw standing before her an old grandmother-woman. The girl asked the woman, "I am so lost. Can you help me?"

"Of course I will, child. Come in from the cold!" **[it will be funnier if you as a man pretend to be an old woman- the funny things make this story safer for younger children]** said the old woman.

When the girl entered the house, she sat down next to the fire. She opened up her sack to eat her meal.

"Oh," said the old woman, "I have not eaten much today. Would you share your snack with me?'

The little girl agreed and said, **[you can sound like a little girl if you really want to play]** "Here, take what you want and I will eat what is left over."**[reach out your hands out as if you are offering the food to the old woman]**

When the grandmother had eaten some of the food, the girl ate her portion of the bread and jelly. There was even some left over.

"Well," said the kindly old woman, "it is not safe for you to go back out into the darkness to find your way home. You should stay here for the night. You may sleep in my soft bed in my room **[point with one hand towards the room and with the other hand out to the straw on the ground]** and I will sleep out here on some straw on the floor."

"No, I will take the straw and you can stay in your soft bed. Your old bones deserve a soft place to sleep." **[the little girl could pat the old woman on the shoulder- show this by patting your child on the shoulder- touching your kids in storytelling is a good thing]** the girl responded.

So they slept the night away. When the girl woke up **[yawn and stretch]** in the morning, she could not find the old woman anywhere. **[pretend to look around]** However, at the front door, there was a **[pause]** large **[pause]** sack **[pause]** of gold coins and a note attached to it **[show surprise in your face, voice and eyes]**.

The note read **[read the note in the same voice of the old woman- hold out your hands as if the note were in it]** , "Dear Child, I am an enchanted fairy who needed someone to be kind to her. Because of your kindness, I have given you this bag of gold. On the other side of this note, you will find the map to guide you out of the forest. Thank you and live a long happy life."

The girl took the map and the gold **[let the girl grunt as she picks up the heavy sack]** and set out to her home. When she arrived at her house, her family was happy to see that she was safe and sound. She told them the story of what had happened and showed them the bag of gold.

[the story now repeats the same pattern except this time all the opposite things happen and this rude sister speaks in a mean way for all her lines] Her sister heard this story and was very jealous **[narrow your eyes and talk through your teeth as you say that line]**. So, she packed **[throw things in the**

imaginary sack] up a bag of delicious snacks and set out to find the old woman's house.

As night fell, the sister found the old woman's house, with the light from the fire shining through the windows. The sister banged **[before you had pretended to knock, now bang on the door]** on the door.

When the old woman answered, the sister demanded to be let in. The old woman agreed.

The sister then began to eat her snacks. As before, the old woman asked to have some of the meal. The sister replied **[be mean but exaggerate it so that your child knows you are playing- our male voices can be too strong unless we are clearly playing]**, "I have been walking all day and I am very hungry. You can have what is left over."

However, the sister was rude and she ate nearly every last piece of the snacks, leaving just crumbs and bits left for the old woman.

When it was time for bed, the old woman again offered to sleep on the straw **[repeat the pointing as you did the first time]** while the sister could have the bed. Then, without even a concern for the old woman's weary body, the sister ran to the bedroom **[use your hands to show running]**, slammed **[say the word "slammed" the way it sounds when you slam a door]** the door and slept all night on the soft bed **[maybe make some snoring sounds]**, while the old woman had to sleep on the straw.

In the morning **[yawn and stretch]**, the rude sister was eager to see her reward. Of course, the old woman was gone, but the sister could not care less about that. On the floor was a note and a **[pause]** very **[pause]** small **[pause]** bag. The rude sister grabbed **[pretend to grab the note- you should say "grabbed" quick and fast just like the gesture looks]** the note to read it.

"Dear child," the note began, "I have put the map on the back of this note to guide you back home. As well, you will find the reward that you deserve in this small sack. You should open it at once!"

When the rude sister opened the bag, there was no gold inside of [show surprise] it. Instead, there was a bird with a sharp beak, which flew out of the bag and grabbed the sister's nose [this scene should be spoken quickly and with surprise-play with the gestures and the image of stretching the nose]. The bird pulled harder and harder and the girl's nose stretched longer and longer [the word "longer" should be drawn out as if you were stretching out the word]. It pulled so hard that her nose hung all the way down to her feet [point down to the ground]. Then the bird vanished, leaving the sister with the long nose.

The long-nosed sister made her way home, tripping over her nose and being laughed at by everyone she passed, each laugh reminding her how she had been so mean to the old woman.

When she arrived home and shared her story, her family was shocked and amazed at her misfortune. However, as time went by the girl who acted with kindness taught her rude sister how to be kind. With each act of kindness she performed, her nose shrank [as you say this sentence, start with your finger a few inches away from your nose and slowly bring it closer to your nose] just a little bit, until one day, her nose was as normal as normal could be.

Chapter Six

Apples for the Princess

Honesty and Kindness

Background

I have adapted this story from a very long European folktale.[9] You will be able to use this story with any age group.

The Story

When the princess was very sick, the king would do anything to help her get better. The doctors said the only thing  that could make her better was a bushel of perfect yellow apples brought to her by the most honest and kind young man in the great kingdom.

The king sent out proclamations to every corner of his kingdom. Some young men brought perfect apples, but in their hearts they were not very nice people.

A farmer with three sons heard of the proclamation and decided that his oldest son was the one to take a bushel of their most perfect apples to the princess. The farmer filled the basket with apples and covered it with a thick blanket. He sent the oldest boy on his way to the castle and told him not to delay or talk to anyone until he got there.

On the way, the oldest son met an old, hairy man on the road. The boy did not know the man was a wizard. The man called out, "What do you have in the basket, son?"

The oldest son looked at the old man and immediately decided the old man was not worthy of a serious answer. The boy rudely blurted out to the man, "My basket is full of frogs, you fool."

The hairy man looked at him and said, "Well as you say, so it is."

When the oldest son arrived at the castle, he was immediately let in to see the princess. When he took the blanket off of his bushel basket, the apples were gone and hundreds of frogs came leaping out. With the castle filled with frogs, the king banished the oldest son and sent him on his way back home.

When the oldest son arrived home, he shared his story with his father and his brothers. The farmer then decided to send the middle son on his way, with a bushel of perfect apples covered with a thick blanket.

On his way, the middle son met the same hairy man. When the hairy man asked about the contents of the basket, the middle son very rudely told him, "I have baby piglets in this basket, you smelly old man."

The old man looked at the rude boy and said, "Well as you say, so it is."

So, too, when the middle son arrived to see the princess the guards let him enter the hall. When he took the blanket off the basket, hundreds of baby pigs ran out and filled up every room in the castle. The king also banished this son to his home.

When the middle son arrived home, the farmer thought his days of princess-curing were through. The youngest son asked the father if he could go to the castle with some apples. Although the farmer thought his youngest son was a fool, he did give him a basket of perfect apples covered with a thick blanket.

When the boy met the hairy man on the road, he too heard the question, "What do you have in your basket, son?"

"Good day, old man! I have a basket full of perfect apples that will make the princess well again!" the boy replied.

The hairy man looked at the boy and smiled. He said to him, "Well as you say, so it is." He waved the youngest son on towards the castle.

When the youngest son arrived at the castle, the guards let him in to see the princess. He took the blanket off the basket and revealed the most perfect, shining, delicious apples anyone had ever seen- a reward for the boy's kindness and honesty to the hairy wizard man. The princess took one bite and was immediately cured of her illness. The entire kingdom was very happy.

In case you want to know, after many adventures the youngest son and the princess decided to be married. At their wedding, they served a delicious apple cake to all their guests.

Your "Brick-And-Mortar Story Reminder"™ List

1. Ill princess needs yellow apples brought by kind young man
2. King issues request and young men arrive at castle
3. Some unkind young men bring perfect apples
4. Farmer sends first son with perfect apples
5. First son meets hairy man and says he has frogs in basket
6. "Well as you say, so it is." says the hairy man
7. First son arrives at castle and basket is filled with many frogs
8. Second son is sent to the castle with more apples
9. Second son meets man, says his basket has piglets in it
10. "Well as you say, so it is." says the hairy man

11. Second son arrives at castle, basket is filled with many piglets
12. Third son is sent to castle with more apples
13. Third son meets hairy man and politely says he has apples
14. "Well as you say, so it is." says the hairy man
15. Third son arrives at castle with perfect apples
16. Princess eats apple and is cured
17. Son and Princess marry, perfect apple cake at wedding

My Coaching Notes for You

[once again, do not get stressed about the length of this story- the pattern is easy to remember] When the princess [change genders in this story if you want] was very sick, the king would do anything to help her get better. The doctors said the only thing that could make her better was a bushel of perfect [emphasize the need for perfect] yellow apples brought to her by the most honest and kind young man in the great kingdom.

The king sent out proclamations [many stories use words like that your children may not know- explain or ask them to guess] to every corner of his kingdom. Some young men [yes, it could be daughters and the prince is ill- mix the genders as you prefer] brought perfect apples, but in their hearts they were not very nice people.

A farmer with three sons heard of the proclamation and decided that his oldest son was the one to take a bushel of their most perfect apples to the princess. The farmer filled [gesture as if you are filling a basket] the basket with apples and covered it with a thick blanket. He sent the oldest boy on his way to the castle and told him not to delay or talk to anyone [wag your finger at the boy] until he got there.

On the way, the oldest son met an old, hairy [you can describe the man with any adjective you want such as tall, old, skinny, fat, crazy and so forth] man on the road. The boy did not know the man was a wizard. The man called out [use a goofy voice for the hairy man if you want] , "What do you have in the basket, son?"

The oldest son looked at the old man and immediately decided the old man was not worthy of a serious answer [it should be easy for you to know how to talk like the first two boys as you were once a crabby, impatient teenage boy who thought he knew everything]. The boy rudely blurted out to the man, "My basket is full of frogs, you fool."

The hairy man looked at him [a goofy voice here is a good idea] and said [it is best if the hairy man just says this without any anger or frustration], "Well [this means "like you say"] as you say, so it is." [this is the first story in this book where you need to remember to say this phrase the same way every time- even if you do not use the exact words here, always use the same words you have chosen]

When the oldest son arrived at the castle, he was immediately let in to see the princess. When he took the blanket off of his bushel basket, the apples were gone and hundreds of frogs came leaping out [here is your chance to play with the images of frogs jumping everywhere- use your hands and body to indicate jumping and leaping]. With the castle filled with frogs, the king banished the oldest son [use a firm pointing gesture to point the boy out of the castle] and sent him on his way back home.

When the oldest son arrived home, he shared his story with his father the farmer and his brothers [boy should hang his head as he talks]. The farmer then decided to send the middle son on his way, with a bushel of perfect apples covered with a thick blanket [pretend to throw the blanket over the basket].

On his way, the middle son met the same hairy man. When the hairy man asked about the contents of the basket, the middle son very rudely told him [here you are again, remembering to speak like you did when you were an 18 year old boy and knew everything], "I have baby piglets in this basket, you smelly old man."

The old man looked at the rude boy and said, "Well as you say, so it is." **[remember this phrase should be the same as the last time you used it]**

So, too, when the middle son arrived to see the princess the guards let him enter the hall. When he took the blanket off the basket, hundreds of baby pigs **[little children love the idea of baby pigs so play with this image and have fun]** ran out and filled up every room in the castle **[make some baby pig snorts and squeals]**. The king also banished this son back to his home.

When the middle son arrived home, the farmer thought his days of princess curing were through. The youngest son asked the father if he could go to the castle with some apples. Although the farmer thought his youngest son was a fool **[make a big sigh as if the farmer dad is just not sure about sending this last boy out]**, he did give him a basket of perfect apples covered with a thick blanket.

When the boy met the hairy man on the road, he too heard the question, "What do you have in your basket, son?"

[the boy should just speak with some excitement to the man] "Good day, old man! I have a basket full of perfect apples that will make the princess well again!" the boy replied.

The hairy man looked at the boy and smiled. He said to him, "Well as you say, so it is." **[here you are using the same phrase as before- after you tell this story to your children a few times, they will be able to say this with you]** He waved the youngest son on towards the castle.

When the youngest son arrived at the castle, the guards let him in to see the princess. He took the blanket off the basket and revealed **[pause]** the most perfect, shining, delicious apples anyone had ever seen- a reward for the boy's kindness and honesty to the hairy wizard man. The princess took one bite and was immediately cured of her illness. The entire kingdom was very happy.

In case you want to know **[say this like you are sharing a secret]**, after many adventures the youngest son and the princess decided to be married. At their wedding, they served a delicious apple cake to all their guests.

Chapter Seven

The Lion and the Mouse

Self-Worth

Background

You have probably heard this story in many places. Here is a simple version for your bedtime telling.[10]

The Story

WHOMP! The lion's paw fell straight down and landed on top of the little mouse. The lion looked at the mouse and decided that he should eat the mouse as his mid-day snack.

"Please don't eat me," said the mouse "for if you let me go I will someday be able to help you, great lion!"

The lion thought the idea of the tiny little mouse helping him was so funny that he laughed out loud. Then he let the mouse go as he was laughing so hard he could not eat. As the mouse ran away, the sound of the lion laughing faded away into the background.

A few days later, the very same lion was hunting in the jungle when he came upon a big pile of tasty meat, which was his favorite food. As he stepped closer to the meat, he triggered a trap that swept him up in a huge net made of rough rope.

Just at that moment, the mouse walked past where the lion was trapped. The lion called out for the mouse to help him.

The mouse began to chew on the rope net until it broke apart and the lion was free of the trap.

"See, I told you that I would someday help you," said the mouse to the lion. And from that day on, the great lion never forgot how even the smallest creature could be very helpful.

Your "Brick-And-Mortar Story Reminder"™ List

1. Lion's paw lands on little mouse
2. Lion plans on eating mouse
3. Mouse asks to be set free, promises to help lion someday
4. Lion laughs at idea and lets mouse run away free
5. Later, lion is caught in a trap
6. Mouse finds lion, chews ropes until lion is set free
7. Mouse "See I told you…"
8. Lion amazed that a small creature could help

My Coaching Notes for You

WHOMP! The lion's paw fell straight down and landed on top of the little mouse **[make this a quick gesture as your hand lands on top of the bed, couch or your child's head to catch the mouse]**. The lion **[in some versions of this story, the mouse is running around the sleeping lion before he gets caught]** looked at the mouse **[you could hold your hand as if you were dangling the mouse from his tail or make a fist with the mouse's head sticking out of the top]** and decided that he **[change genders if you want]** should eat the mouse as his mid-day snack.

"Please don't eat me" **[really play with this short story, starting with the way the little mouse talks- you can't go wrong by having fun]**, said the mouse "for if you let me go I will someday be able to help you, great lion!"

The lion thought the idea **[maybe mutter a "hmmm" and scratch your chin]** of the tiny little **[remember that small children love the idea of tiny things]** mouse helping him was so funny that he laughed out loud [make a big laugh here]. Then he let the mouse go as he was laughing so hard he could not eat.

As the mouse ran away [use your finger to show the zig zag path of the mouse running away], the sound of the lion laughing faded away into the background.

A few days later, the very same lion was hunting [look about side to side pretending to hunt] in the jungle when he came upon a big pile of tasty meat [rub your hands on your child's head, pretending it is the pile of meat- you should get some giggles from your child- play with this as long as you want], which was his favorite food. As he stepped closer to the meat, he triggered a trap that swept him up [say this quickly] in a huge net made of rough rope [swing your hands back and forth, like the lion swinging away in the rope-net trap].

Just at that moment, the mouse walked [use your hand again to indicate the mouse walking along in a zig-zag pattern] past where the lion was trapped. The lion called out for the mouse to help him [you can make up a conversation here between the lion and mouse- take turns with your child as you both pretend to be lion or mouse] . The mouse began to chew on the rope net until it finally broke apart and the lion was free of the trap.

"See, I told you that I would someday help you," said the mouse to the lion. And from that day on, the great lion never forgot how even the smallest creature could be very helpful [when telling stories that have a moral attached, just say the moral in your normal, everyday voice- avoid the "now, you need to learn this" voice].

Chapter Eight

The Stag at the Pool

Self-Worth

Background

This quick story, adapted from a world-fable[11], is a good choice for your older children who may have outgrown the "lion and mouse" story in the previous chapter. I bet you were thinking this "stag" might be about a party you had in your bachelor days. Sorry, it's not. Like all stories, however, you can adapt this to fit any age. Just play around with it. You won't go wrong in making a story to fit your unique child.

The Story

At the end of a long run, a stag (that is a male deer) came to a lake to drink and quench his thirst. As he drank, he saw his

reflection in the water. He admired his giant antlers, thinking how powerful they made him seem.

He then noticed his thin legs and tiny feet. "What good are those skinny legs? I wish they were as perfect as my antlers," he thought.

Just at that moment, he heard a twig snap behind

him. There were hunters coming at him. With his strong legs, he quickly jumped and ran away as fast as he could.

The hunters continued to chase him until he took refuge in a thicket of trees. However, his antlers got caught in the trees and he could not escape the hunters. He thought to himself, "What a fool I am. I admired my antlers, which have only caused me this problem when it was my small feet and skinny legs that would do me the most good."

(Note: If you want to change the ending, you can let the Stag escape in just the nick of time. For older children, the idea that vanity and not understanding or appreciating our gifts can result in harm is not a bad message to teach. You decide.)

Your "Brick-And-Mortar Story Reminder"™ List

1. Stag is running and comes to the lake to drink
2. Stag sees his antlers in reflection and thinks they are terrific
3. Stag notices small legs and thinks they are bad
4. Stag hears hunters coming and runs away with his strong legs
5. Stag runs into bushes, gets antlers caught in bushes
6. Realizes that his antlers are not as useful as his legs
7. Your option to have stag escape or be caught

My Coaching Notes for You

At the end of a long run, a stag (that is a male deer) **[describing the deer as a stag is part of the vocabulary building benefits of storytelling]** came to a lake to drink and quench his thirst **[quench is another unusual word for some kids]**. As he drank, he saw his reflection in the water. He admired his giant antlers, thinking how powerful they made him seem.

He then noticed his thin legs and tiny feet. "What good are those skinny legs? I wish they were as perfect as my antlers," [for a simple story like this told to older children, use your normal, conversational voice] he thought.

Just at that moment, he heard a twig snap [the word "snap" should be said quickly while snapping your fingers] behind him. There were hunters coming at him. With his strong legs, he quickly jumped and ran away as fast as he could [make a gesture here with your hand that shows moving quickly forward].

The hunters continued to chase him until he took refuge in a thicket of trees. However, his antlers got caught in the trees [grab your head with your hands] and he could not escape the hunters. He thought to himself, "What a fool I am. I admired my antlers, which have only caused me this problem when it was my small feet and skinny legs that would do me the most good." [you need to decide which ending you will use- however part of the good thing about this story is it helps your older kids understand that the world is not always fair- happy and unhappy endings are a part of life]

Chapter Nine

The Ant and the Dove

Self-Worth and Kindness

Background

I use this story often to illustrate the idea that even the smallest kindness can be repaid many times over. As well, in this world fable[12], we can see that the littlest being can help out. This idea will be very popular with your small children.

The Story

The little ant loved to take long walks along the river. One

day, when the wind was very strong, the little ant was blown right into the rushing river water. The ant could not swim, so he began to cry out for help.

Flying high above was a dove who heard the screams for help. The dove landed right on the bank of the river and saw the little ant screaming for help. The dove picked up a small twig in its beak and threw the twig out to the ant. The ant was able to climb up on the twig and float away to safety.

The dove didn't think about the ant much more and flew back to wherever he was going to go.

Some time later, the very same ant was walking along through the forest and saw right before him a hunter who had his bow and arrow pointed right at the very same dove who had helped the ant so many days ago.

Wanting to help the dove, the ant quickly ran up to the big hunter's foot, opened his little jaws and bit the hunter hard on the foot. This made the hunter scream in pain and drop his bow and arrow.

The dove heard the hunter yelling, saw that his life was in danger and quickly flew away. The dove was happy to know that his little bit of kindness had been returned, even from a creature as teeny-tiny as the ant.

Your "Brick-And-Mortar Story Reminder"™ List

1. Ant walking along river
2. Wind blows the ant into river and ant cannot swim
3. Dove above hears the cries and lands next to river
4. Dove throws twig in water and ant is saved from drowning
5. Later, ant walks through the forest
6. Ant sees hunter with arrow aimed at dove
7. Ant bites hunter with jaws and hunter drops bow
8. Dove hears scream, flies away to safety
9. Dove is happy that his kindness is repaid by little creature

My Coaching Notes for You

The little ant loved to take long walks along the river. One day, when the wind was very strong, the little **[with small children emphasize the ant's size]** ant was blown right into the rushing river water. The ant could not swim, so he began to cry out for help. **[pretend to sound like the ant crying out for help]**

Flying high above was a dove who heard the screams for help. The dove landed right on the bank of the river **[you could use your hands to indicate the dove landing]** and saw the little ant screaming for help. The dove picked up a small twig in its beak and threw **[give a little grunt when the twig is thrown]** the twig out to the ant. The ant was able to climb up on the twig and float away to safety.

The dove didn't think about the ant much more and flew **[use your hands again to indicate the dove flying up]** back to wherever he was going to go.

Some time later, the very same ant was walking along through the forest and saw right before him a hunter **[look and point up to show the ant's perspective from down on the ground]** who had his bow and arrow pointed right at **["what do you think the hunter was aiming at?"]** the very same dove who had helped the ant so many days ago.

Wanting to help the dove, the ant quickly ran up to the big hunter's foot, opened his little jaws and bit **[make it sound like the ant is taking a great big bite]** the hunter hard on the foot. This made the hunter scream in pain **[you could make a funny scream here]** and drop his bow and arrow.

The dove heard the hunter yelling, saw that his life was in danger and quickly flew away **[hand motion of the dove flying away]**. The dove was happy to know that his little bit of kindness had been returned, even from a creature as teeny-tiny as the ant.

Chapter Ten

The Fisherman and His Wife

The Danger of Greed

Background

I have adapted[13] for you an old tale about how greed can make you crazy. It is probably the most complicated story in this volume of the DaddyTeller™ series. Take your time to learn it.

The Story

Once upon a time there was a fisherman who was a very

good fisherman. He loved to go out and fish each day, leaving his simple, tiny house behind as he jumped into his boat and sailed off to catch fish.

However, his wife Isabel was not happy at all. She wanted more and more things and could never be happy just enjoying the sunshine and fresh food she had each day.

One day, the fisherman went out to fish and cast his line into the sea. He waited and waited for something to bite when suddenly there was a huge tug on his line. He pulled up his fishing line and what fell into his boat was a big, flat fish called a flounder. It was huge! The fisherman thought to himself how happy he would be when he sat down at the table to eat this delicious fish with his wife whom he loved so much.

Just as he was dreaming of this great meal, the fish looked up at the fisherman and began to speak. "Fisherman," said the fish, "I am an enchanted prince who has been turned into a fish. If you set me free, I will grant you any wish you want."

The fisherman was amazed to see this talking fish. "I am so lucky to have found a talking fish!" he said with great excitement. "And, I am already happy with my house, my wife and my life, there is nothing more I could wish for. So, I am glad to send you back to the water! Goodbye, fish!"

And with those words, the fisherman threw the fish back into the water. He then took his boat home to his little house.

When he told his wife what had happened, she yelled at him. "What? You had a fish that would grant you a wish and you threw it back? You go back to the water and you tell that fish you have a wish to have a great big house! Do you understand me, husband?"

1. So, the next morning the fisherman set out. When he got to the water, the day was crystal clear and the water smooth. The fisherman called out,

"Oh fish, oh fish, out in the sea! Come and hear my humble plea! Isabel, my wedded wife, doesn't like our way of life!"

Suddenly, the fish stuck his head out of the water and asked what the fisherman wanted.

Said the fisherman, "My wife is not happy and wants to know if I can still have my wish."

"Yes," the fish said, "you can still have your wish."

The fisherman answered, "Oh, thank you. She would like a much bigger house. Can you give us a bigger house?"

"Yes, I can. Go fisherman, for it is done." And with that, the fish disappeared back under the water.

When the fisherman returned home, he saw that the fish had changed the little house into a great big house with many doors, windows, rooms and stairs. The fisherman's wife was sitting outside.

The fisherman asked her, "Now are you happy?"

"No!" said his wife. "I have a brand new house but no good clothes to wear or food to eat in my new house. You go back and you tell that fish that I want to have new clothes and new food. Do you understand me?"

2. Early the next morning the fisherman set out. When he got to the water, the day was a little cloudy and the water was a bit choppy. The fisherman called out,

"Oh fish, oh fish, out in the sea! Come and hear my humble plea! Isabel, my wedded wife, doesn't like our way of life!"

Suddenly, the fish stuck his head out of the water and asked what the fisherman wanted.

Said the fisherman, "My wife is not happy and wants to know if I can have another wish."

"Yes," the fish said, "you may have another wish."

The fisherman answered, "Oh, thank you. She would like to have fancy new clothes and fancy new food. Can you give her food and clothes?"

"Yes, I can. Go fisherman, for it is done." And with that, the fish disappeared back under the water.

When the fisherman returned home, his wife was sitting outside her house in a dress made with golden thread. In each hand she held a great big turkey leg and was gobbling them down.

The fisherman asked his wife if she was happy.

She said, "No, I am not happy. I want more. I want to be powerful. I want you to tell the fish to make me queen of all the lands. You go back and you tell that fish that I need to be queen. Do you understand me husband?"

3. On the next day, the fisherman set out. When he arrived at the place where he fished, the day was very cloudy,

the wind was blowing and the water had waves in it. The fisherman called out,

"Oh fish, oh fish, out in the sea! Come and hear my humble plea! Isabel, my wedded wife, doesn't like our way of life!"

As before, the fish stuck his head out of the water and asked what the fisherman wanted.

Said the fisherman, "My wife is not happy and wants to know if I can have another wish."

"Yes," the fish sighed, "you may have yet another wish."

The fisherman answered, "Oh, thank you. She would like to be very powerful. She wants to be the queen of all the land!"

"The queen of the land! That is a big wish, fisherman," the fish said.

The fisherman could only look at the fish and sigh.

"Very well, fisherman, I will give her what she wants. Go fisherman, for it is done." And with that, the fish disappeared back under the water.

When the fisherman returned home, his house was gone! In its place was a huge castle. In front of the castle was a long line of people waiting to see the new queen. They were carrying many gifts for the queen. The fisherman got in line with the others so that he could talk to his wife, the new queen.

After a long time of waiting, the fisherman finally arrived in front of the throne of his wife the queen. He asked her if she was, finally, happy.

"No!" said the queen. "I am not happy. I want even more power! I want to oversee everything in the universe! You go back and you tell that fish that I want to be the Sun! Do you understand me, husband?"

The fisherman took a look at his wife, whom he loved very much. But now, he was afraid she had gone just a little crazy.

4. One more time, the fisherman set out to find the magic fish. When he and his boat were at the place where the

fish always came up, the day was starting to storm and the water was very rough and violent. The fisherman called out,

"Oh fish, oh fish, out in the sea! Come and hear my humble plea! Isabel, my wedded wife, doesn't like our way of life!"

Suddenly, the fish stuck his head out of the water and asked what the fisherman wanted.

Said the fisherman, "My wife is not happy and wants to know if I can have another wish."

"Yes," the fish said, "you can have one more wish. What could she possibly need now?"

The fisherman answered, "Oh, thank you. She says she is still not happy, even if I still love her very much. She wants to be the Sun in the heavens. I was wondering if you could 'help' me with this last wish?"

The fish understood what the fisherman wanted him to do. "Yes, I can help you. Go fisherman, for it is. . .done." And with that, the fish disappeared back under the water.

When the fisherman returned home, the castle had vanished! In its place was the simple, nice house that he had always owned. Sitting in front of the house was his wife, dressed in her simple, nice clothes and eating her simple, good food. She looked very surprised. When the fisherman saw her, he loved her even more.

He said to his wife, "Now we can be happy always. Will that be good enough?"

She said to him, "Well, as long as you still love me, yes, I will be happy."

And so, they lived, as always, happily ever after. And they learned that sometimes getting too greedy can make you just very crazy.

Your "Brick-And-Mortar Story Reminder"™ List

This story is the most complex story in this book. As your coach, I want you to know that it will be well worth your time to tell this story to your children; you will feel as if you have completed your first storytelling triathlon. Work as hard on this story as you have on sports, business or other undertakings in your life. Give yourself time to learn it to share it with your children.

Pay attention to the fact that there is a pattern of: wife to fisherman to the sea to the chant to the fish to the request to the results which then starts the process over again. See that in each cycle, the weather changes and the fish and fisherman become a little more frustrated. Once you register at the www.daddyteller.com/extrabook site, you'll be able to hear me tell this story. That will help you to understand the nuances of this story better than reading my notes alone.

1. Fisherman (FM) is happy in small house with his wife.
2. Wife is not happy
3. FM goes to sea and pulls in the fish
4. Fish speaks and offers wish in exchange for being set free
5. FM already has all he needs and throws fish back
6. Wife is angry as wish wasn't asked for, demands new house
7. Pattern: FM goes to sea
   Water/Weather is smooth and clear
   FM sings chant
   Fish appears and FM requests new house with wish
   Fish grants wish: "Go, fisherman, it is done."
   FM returns home
8. New house is not enough and wife wants new food/clothing
9. Pattern: FM goes to sea
   Water/Weather is choppy

FM sings chant

Fish appears and FM requests food/clothing wish

Fish grants wish: "Go, fisherman, it is done."

FM returns home

10. FM sees new food/clothing and wife now wants to be queen

11. Pattern: FM goes to sea

Water/Weather is getting rough

FM sings chant

Fish appears and FM asks for wife's wish to be queen

Fish grants wish: "Go, fisherman, it is done."

FM returns home

12. Being queen is not enough and wife wants to be the sun

13. Pattern: FM goes to sea

Water/Weather is very rough

FM sings chant

Fish appears and FM asks for the fish to "help" him.

Fish understands the meaning of "help"

Fish tells FM that it is "done"

FM returns home

14. FM returns home to find all the fancy things gone.

15. FM asks wife if she is happy, she agrees that she can be

My Coaching Notes for You

Once upon a time there was a happy fisherman who was a very good fisherman. He loved to go out and fish each day, leaving his simple, tiny house **[be sure to mention the simple house]** behind as he jumped into his boat and sailed off to catch fish.

However, his wife Isabel **[you may change the genders of this story and use a name that is easy for you to remember if you would like]** was not happy at all. She wanted more and more things and could never be happy just enjoying the sunshine and fresh food she had each day.

One day, the fisherman went out to fish and cast his line into the sea. He waited and waited for something to bite when suddenly [say the word "suddenly" in a surprised way] there was a huge tug on his line. He pulled up his fishing line and what fell into his boat was a big, flat fish called a flounder [show the size and flatness of the fish with your hands]. It was huge! The fisherman thought to himself how happy he would be when he sat down at the table to eat this delicious fish with his wife whom he loved so much.

Just as he was dreaming of this great meal, the fish looked up at the fisherman and began to speak [does the fish have a funny voice or do you want to just use your normal voice- the choice is yours]. "Fisherman," said the fish, "I am an enchanted prince who has been turned into a fish. If you set me free, I will grant you any wish you want."

The fisherman was amazed to see this talking fish. "I am so lucky to have found a talking fish!"[fisherman is both amazed and delighted- sound happy] he said with great excitement. "And, I am already happy with my house, my wife and my life, there is nothing more I could wish for. So, I am glad to send you back to the water! Goodbye, fish!"

And with those words, the fisherman threw the fish back into the water [remember to play when you exaggerate the fisherman heaving the big fish into the water with a loud splash and a quick wave goodbye with his hands]. He then took his boat home to his little house.

When he told his wife what had happened, she yelled [this yelling should be funny, not a serious drama- open your eyes wide as if the wife wants to stare through the fisherman] at him. "What? You had a fish that would grant you a wish and you threw it back? You go back to the water and you tell that fish you have a wish to have a great big house! Do you understand me, husband?"

[first pattern starts here] So, the next morning the fisherman set out. When he got to the water, the day was crystal clear and the water smooth [the weather changes in the story to indicate that the wishes are getting more and more bizarre-do your best to include these details]. The fisherman called out [although I don't want you to memorize the stories, here I want you to use the same words for this chant every time you tell this story and every time you say it in the story- after a while your children will not be able to stop saying it with you as it is just too much fun]

"Oh fish, oh fish, out in the sea! Come and hear my humble plea! Isabel, my wedded wife, doesn't like our way of life!"

Suddenly, the fish stuck his head out of the water [look around the room like the fish just sticking his big flat head out of the water] and asked what the fisherman wanted.

Said the fisherman, "My wife is not happy and wants to know if I can still have my wish." [at this point the fish and the fisherman are pretty happy and there is no tension]

"Yes," the fish said, "you can still have your wish."

The fisherman answered, "Oh, thank you. She would like a much bigger house. Can you give us a bigger house?"

"Yes, I can. Go fisherman, for it is done." [the word "done" here means that his wish is granted- later the word will have a different meaning] And with that, the fish disappeared back under the water.

When the fisherman returned home, he saw that the fish had changed the little house into a great big house with many doors, windows, rooms and stairs. The fisherman's wife was sitting outside.

The fisherman asked her, "Now are you happy?" [whenever the fisherman asks this question, he really does want her to be happy- he never asks it in a way to put her down or insult her]

"No!" said his wife. "I have a brand new house but no good clothes to wear or food to eat in my new house. You go back and you tell that fish that I want to have new clothes and new food. Do you understand me?" **[I like to make this "understand me" a little more crazy each time she asks it}**

[your second pattern starts here- the ideas of the previous pattern notes apply here- see how the weather changes- don't stress out over the weather if that makes the story too hard for you] Early the next morning the fisherman set out. When he got to the water, the day was a little cloudy and the water was a bit choppy. The fisherman called out,

"Oh fish, oh fish, out in the sea! Come and hear my humble plea! Isabel, my wedded wife, doesn't like our way of life!"

Suddenly, the fish stuck his head out of the water and asked what the fisherman wanted.

Said the fisherman, "My wife is not happy and wants to know if I can have another wish."

"Yes," the fish said, "you may have another wish." **[fish is still willing to help out]**

The fisherman answered, "Oh, thank you. She would like to have fancy new clothes and fancy new food. Can you give her food and clothes?"

"Yes, I can. Go fisherman, for it is done." And with that, the fish disappeared back under the water.

When the fisherman returned home, his wife was sitting outside her house in a dress made with golden thread. In each hand she held a great big turkey leg and was gobbling them down **[the image of the turkey legs can be very funny to your child if you pretend to chomp down on the food]**.

The fisherman asked his wife is she was happy.

She said, "No, I am not happy. I want more. I want to be powerful. I want you to tell the fish to make me queen of all the lands. You go back and you tell that fish that I need to be queen. Do you understand me husband?"

[here again is the next pattern and the weather changes] On the next day, the fisherman set out. When he arrived at the place where he fished, the day was a very cloudy, the wind was blowing and the water had waves in it. The fisherman called out,

"Oh fish, oh fish, out in the sea! Come and hear my humble plea! Isabel, my wedded wife, doesn't like our way of life!"

As before, the fish stuck his head out of the water and asked what the fisherman wanted.

Said the fisherman, "My wife is not happy and wants to know if I can have another wish."

"Yes," the fish sighed, "you may have one more wish." **[you should make the fish sound as if he is tired of this process, but still gives in]**

The fisherman answered, "Oh, thank you. She would like to be very powerful. She wants to be the queen of all the land!" **[shake your head in disbelief]**

"The queen of the land! That is a big wish, fisherman," the fish said.

The fisherman could only look at the fish and sigh.

"Very well, fisherman, I will give her what she wants. Go fisherman, for it is done." And with that, the fish disappeared back under the water.

When the fisherman returned home, his house was gone! In its place was a huge castle. In front of the castle was a long **[you can say the word "long" in a looooonnnngg way]** line of people waiting to see the new queen. They were carrying many gifts for the queen. The fisherman got in line with the others so that he could talk to his wife, the new queen.

After a long time of waiting, the fisherman finally arrived in front of the throne of his wife the queen. He asked her if she was, finally, happy.

"No!" said the queen. "I am not happy. I want even more power! I want to oversee everything in the universe! You go back and you tell that fish that I want to be the Sun! Do you understand me, husband?" **[at this point, you can make the wife speak as if she is completely bonkers]**

The fisherman took a look at his wife, whom he loved very much. But now, he was afraid she had gone just a little crazy **[put your head down with your face in your hands]**.

[here is your last pattern- see how the weather is really rough] One more time, the fisherman set out to find the magic fish. When he and his boat were at the place where the fish always came up, the day was starting to storm and the water was very rough and violent. The fisherman called out,

"Oh fish, oh fish, out in the sea! Come and hear my humble plea! Isabel, my wedded wife, doesn't like our way of life!"

Suddenly, the fish stuck his head out of the water and asked what the fisherman wanted.

Said the fisherman, "My wife is not happy and wants to know if I can have another wish."

"Yes," the fish said, "you can have one more wish. What could she possibly need now?" **[the fish can not believe another wish is being requested- speak this question slowly]**

The fisherman answered, "Oh, thank you. She says she is still not happy, even if I still love her very much. She wants to be the Sun in the heavens. I was wondering if you could 'help' me with this last wish?" **[the fisherman is hoping that the fish understands that he wants the fish to help him end the craziness- put emphasis on the word help]**

The fish understood what the fisherman wanted him to do. "Yes, I can help you. Go fisherman, for it is. . .done." **[the fish here says "done" to mean that the crazy wishes are being taken away and this series of events is finished- when you put the emphasis on how "help" and "done" are said, you're helping your child to learn about the ideas of inflection]** And with that, the fish disappeared back under the water.

When the fisherman returned home, the castle had vanished! In its place was the simple, nice house that he had always owned. **[young children (and some adults) will not always understand why the house has vanished- talk it through with them]** Sitting in front of the house was his wife, dressed in her simple, nice clothes and eating her simple, good food. She looked very surprised. When the fisherman saw her, he loved her even more.

He said to his wife, "Now we can be happy always. Will that be good enough?" **[the voice you use for the fisherman is not mad at his wife- he wants her to be happy but not crazy with greed]**

She said to him, "Well, as long as you still love me, yes, I will be happy."

And so, they lived, as always, happily ever after. And they learned that sometimes getting too greedy can make you just very crazy **[this story is a lot of fun to tell especially as your children join in and start to learn the sequence of events- do not worry if they are "getting it" or not].**

Chapter Eleven

A Word to Mom

I want to take a moment in this last chapter to talk to the Mother of your children. Call her on over and let me "speak" to her (Hint: You should read this, too.).

Dear Mom- in our world today, there is a lot of support for being a Mommy and well there should be. However, the support for being a Daddy is nearly impossible to find. I know that for some Dads, this may be the only book that they have ever seen about communicating directly with their children.

I have to ask you a favor. Let the DaddyTeller™ man in your life do this storytelling in his own way, with his way of talking and style. You might have a whole list of ways he could "do it better." But, unless he asks you, don't offer the advice. The relationship he has formed with his child is unique. It should and must be different from the relationship you have with the child. It will sound different, look different, feel different.

Mom, if you start digging in to "help" him, he's going to give up this important fathering task. I am a man and I have worked with men and boys for a lot of years. I know how we think and how our pride needs to just let us figure it out for ourselves. It's a guy thing. Trust me, when he has a question for you, he'll ask it.

The DaddyTeller™ man you have in your life is going to tell a story differently than it is written in this book. He is not going to use all the coaching notes I have written out. That is okay. As he gets more comfortable, he is going to make things up, completely changing the story. Through all of this, your child is going to love these storytimes.

I also want you to know that I hope *you* pick up these stories and tell them in your own voice. The same rules apply to him when you are telling. Dad, keep your opinions to yourself as she tells the stories.

About the Author

K. Sean Buvala (www.seantells.net) is a full-time, award-winning pro storyteller. He is the father of four daughters and the husband of one wife. When he is not on the road teaching and training, he is home in the greater Phoenix, Arizona area. His wife says he is a great cook, as well.

When he is not telling stories to his children or telling at local schools, he works with businesses, non-profit groups and entrepreneurs to teach them to grow their bottom line and employee satisfaction via the power of storytelling and narrative.

Sean is also the director of Storyteller.net, an international resource for both those who tell stories and those who love to hear stories. Storyteller.net is one of the original Internet sites devoted to storytelling, actually having been around longer than everybody's favorite googly[14] search engine.

To book Sean to speak to or coach your group about the DaddyTeller™ project or any aspect of storytelling for your company, please contact him via Email at sean@storyteller.net. Include a subject line that indicates the nature of your request.

If you are a Twitter™ user, you may also reach Sean by following him @storyteller. Also, please follow @daddyteller for more news, tips and tricks.

Coming Soon!

DaddyTeller™ Volume Two:
How to Be a Hero to Your Kids and
Teach Them What's Really Important
By Telling One Simple Story at a Time.

Including:
*New stories to support the teaching of more values
*Special chapters on telling DaddyTeller™ stories of your
own childhood (without sounding like a dork) and the
things you learned when you were "their age."

Be sure to register at the website to get
information in advance about volume two!
http://www.daddyteller.com/extrabook.
Your password is: mouselion2apple.

How About the DaddyTeller™ Author Speak At Your Event for Little or No Cost?

We would be happy to work with you to create bulk sales of this book that you can give away or sell to members of your group, church, school or other organization.

Based on the number of books you buy, you can reduce or eliminate the costs of having Sean speak or train at your event.

To learn more, send an Email to staff@daddyteller.com and put the words "Bulk Booking" in the subject line.

We are looking forward to having Sean be a part of your event.

End Notes

[1] This book is great for Moms, too. However, we are using some "guy speak" in this series and you will just have to adjust to that. I am happy to help any parent, regardless of gender, learn to communicate their values to their children.

[2] I use the words "kid," "kids," "child," and "children" interchangeably in this book.

[3] "How Much Time Do Kids Spend with Dad? - Brief Article". USA Today (Society for the Advancement of Education). FindArticles.com. 28 http://findarticles.com/p/articles/mi_m1272/is_2663_129/ai_63986720

[4] For even more advice on these stories, check the www.daddyteller.com website often. While you are there, sign up for the newsletter and we will let you know when updates are released to the website.

[5] I know that some of you reading this book are known as Grandpa, Abuelo, Gramps, Pappy or some other name. My father at first insisted that his grandchildren call him "Mr. Buvala." I think he was only half kidding. Of course, the grandchildren gleefully ignored his request. Whatever name you are called by, I am glad you are reading this book for your grandkids.

[6] I created this story for you from an Aesop fable. All of the stories in this book are meant to be told to your child, not read. Because of that, the writing may seem very simple or not sophisticated. That is okay- work on telling the story, not reading it.

[7] This is also an adaptation from an Aesop fable. In the original, the donkey wears the skin of a dead lion. You might be able to use that idea for older children if you wish.

[8] I created this story from a much longer version written by the Brothers Grimm. You can find it under the title, "St. Joseph in the Forest." A few people may be uncomfortable with some of the ideas in this story such as being alone in the forest and trusting strangers. You will have to decide if your child is ready for this story. You are in charge, Dad.

[9] This story comes from a very long Grimm fairytale titled, "The Griffin." I have adapted it for you to make a perfect DaddyTeller™ bedtime story.

[10] Little children love hearing stories of how small creatures help big creatures. In the classic Aesop tale I have adapted for you, the mouse serves the lion.

[11] This is my take on the Aesop fable of the same name. If you have a child who is just standing at the entrance to adolescence, this story is a great support for when you need to talk about body image.

[12] This, too, is an Aesop fable. The image of the little ant opening his jaws to take a big bite out of the foot can be very funny for your child. Ironically, I most often use this story for my corporate or non-profit management training courses, not for telling to children. You can learn more about those at www.getmorefunding.com .

[13] This tale I adapted from a Brother's Grimm fairytale of the same name. I put this longer tale last in this volume of the DaddyTeller™ book knowing that it might take a bit more time for you to get it down. Take your time to learn it. Numbers printed (like this) are to help you find your place when you are learning the story.

[14] A "googly" is a way of throwing the ball in the game of Cricket. Betcha' didn't know that.